Aryla Publishing © 2020

www.arylapublishing.com

Visit the site for more information on books by

Pamela Malcolm *and to be informed of **free promotions!***

BLACK

is ME

By Pamela Malcolm

Dad, I have a question burning inside of me

I need answers, a reply, response to my enquiry

Why do I wake up each morning with fear in my heart?

Even though I pray, brush my teeth and dress smart

Eat my breakfast, put my school bag on my back

I am still scared. Is it because I am black?

Stepping out of the house, sitting at the back of the bus

I am on my way to school, a place I feel I can trust

As a kid, why do some teachers have me under inspection?

Why, when they are meant to be my protection,

I still get pushed around by bullies who remain

undisciplined

Why is this? Is it because I am black skinned?

If I pitch ideas in a school football team or social club,

Though as talented as I am, it gets dropped

And if I apply to join another group

I have to prove myself more to be approved

School has closed for the day, with my bag on my back,

I am still petrified. Is it because I am black?

I decided to walk home with my friends

A group hanging out of school children

Sirens blazing, the police screaming

Freeze!!! Startled, my hands raised while kneeling

Why did the police release my friends and had me detained?

I am panicking. Is my skin stained?

My child! You must listen to me

Don't be moved by what people see

The sun radiates on your skin,

The moon is envious of your melanin

You are a blessing

Because you are black skinned

Your colour is mesmerizing

Reminds me of the rich taste of coffee

You are a black diamond

Unique, one of a kind in a thousand

You beautify the world with your colour

Being black skinned is an honour

You are a race exhibiting confidence and endurance

You are not swayed by injustice and disturbance

You are proud and powerful like the panther

Kind, warm always bursting with laughter

Full lips, gentle heart with curly hair

You don't despair even when others stare

My Child! Be proud of your heritage

No matter how the world is damaged

Know that you are free and cannot be caged

The whole world is your stage

Keep your head up, don't hold back

You are blessed because you are black

WE ARE ONE Book Series

Other Titles

Thank you for reading……..

Please remember to leave a review if you enjoyed my book it would be nice to hear what you and your children thought of this book☺

Thank you for your time.

Pamela

New Book Series!

For siblings learning to get along its ok to like different things.

Our Giant Pancakes

Playing Farmers

Making Sandcastles

Bathtime Fun

Alien's in Lockdown

Billy Stays Home

*(a coronavirus special)

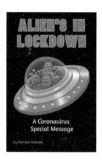 

If you enjoyed this book please also check out these books in the Billy, Ruby and Emergency Services Series below…….

   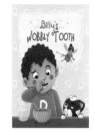 

   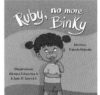 

Alien's in Lockdown
(a Coronavirus Special)

With FREE YouTube video here
=>> https://bit.ly/alienslockdownvid

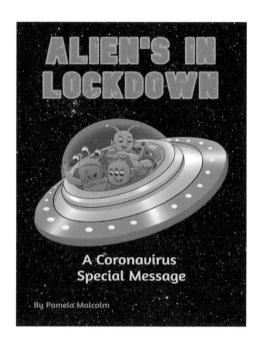

Please visit Aryla Publishing for more books by Pamela Malcolm and other great Authors. Sign up to be informed of upcoming free book promotions and a chance to win prizes in our monthly prize draw.

Please visit Aryla Publishing
and Follow us on Facebook & Instagram
Thank you for your support!

Other children series published by
Aryla Publishing
Author Casey L Adams
Body Goo 1 Sneezing
Body Goo 2 Burping
Body Goo 3 Farting
Body Goo 4 Vomiting
Body Goo 5 The Crusty Bits
Body Goo 6 The Sticky Bits
Love Bugs Don't Step on The Ant
Love Bugs Don't Splat the Spiders
Love Bugs Don't Swat the Bee

Visit **www.ArylaPublishing.com**

to find out about all new releases.

Follow us @arylapublishing on Twitter Instagram & Facebook

Coming Soon.........

Billy Goes To The Zoo

Also _Subscribe_ to Billy's Monthly Vlog on

to find out what he is up to.

New Vlogs monthly

Color In Fun
Kids Books

Other Coloring Books from Aryla Publishing

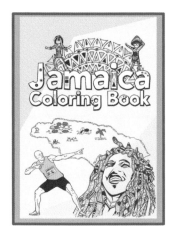

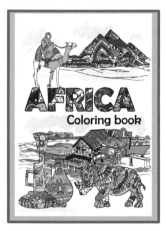

.

Printed in Great Britain
by Amazon

65200945R00015